Long Distance Relationships

How to Maintain a Successful Long Distance Relationship

1

Table of Contents

Introduction

I want to thank you and congratulate you for purchasing the book *'Long Distance Relationships: How to Maintain a Successful Long Distance Relationship"*. This book will be your guide to make your long distance relationship work.

A love relationship is not only about roses, but also about its thorns. While falling in love might be the easier thing to do, keeping a relationship alive can be demanding. But, it gets even more difficult if the two lovers are separated by miles of distance. One needs to constantly work on the relationship. There can be many issues and problems that can threaten a long distance relationship. Issues, such as jealousy and insecurity constantly hover around such a relationship. A deep understanding of them will help you to avoid them at the first place and deal with them effectively if you get to face them. Along with love, the right intention and lots of hard work is required to head in the right direction in the relationship. It is imperative that the one constantly works on the relationship. While it can be difficult, it is definitely not impossible. With some dedicated efforts and some tips, you will do just fine.

If you also share a long distance relationship with your partner, then this book will be your best friend. This book contains some strategies and tips that you can follow to understand the ups and downs that can haunt your long distance relationship. The book lists some tips on how you can work for a successful relationship, in spite of the distance. It also throws some light on the loneliness aspect of such a relationship and talks about ways to deal with it. These tips and strategies will go a long way in helping you to deal with your relationship and to do your best to make it work.

Chapter 1: The Issues of a Long Distance Relationship

A long distance relationship has its own share of issues and problems. While each couple has its own specific problems, there are a few common problems that all of them have to go through. If you want a happy and pleasant long distance relationship, then you should also understand the problems and issues that hover over a long distance relationship. There are many problems that can threaten such a relationship. An understanding of these problems will help you to avoid them or find a solution to them. But, before you think of the probable solutions, you should know of the probable issues that can hit your relationship. Following are few points that can help you understand the issues that lurk over a long distance relationship so that you can avoid them and maintain the zing and the love in your relationship:

1. **Jealousy** – Jealousy is something which needs to be addressed on time, else it can grow beyond bounds. Jealousy could be there because you love your partner very much and are scared to lose him. Or, you could be there because you just simply miss him a lot and don't know how to express it. Whatever may be the case, it is not a healthy emotion because it can complicate many things. From jealousy arises the feeling where you might want to overpower and control your partner. This is not a great thing, so it is better to identify the root cause of your jealousy and eliminate it. In a long distance relationship, it is all the more important to avoid this culprit because from a far distance there is nothing much you would be able to do, except boil your blood for no reason.

2. **Insecurity** – Insecurity can get the better of partners in a long distance relationship. A partner can feel insecure due to many reasons, but the entire reasons boil down to one cause of

not being together. You could be insecure because you miss your partner too much, or you could be insecure because you feel that someone else will be there in his town to compensate for your absence. When you are insecure, you might end up suffocating your partner by not giving him the space and time that he requires. Each person should get his space to function properly. Insecurity takes the form of uncontrollable rage and anger, which is detrimental for both you and your partner. An insecure relationship goes nowhere. And, an insecure person will make the other person miserable and the relationship unstable.

3. **Too many Fights** – Though disagreements and fights are normal in any relationships, but in a long distance relationship, such fights are all the more troubling. The mere fact that you can't see each other will make it very difficult. Fighting over text messages or even a phone call is not the most pleasant thing. The inability to explain your self clearly can intensify the fight. While you can fight and scream at each

other on the phone, you can't hug each other after the fight is over. So, it is difficult to get a sense of peace. Not knowing how the other person is taking the fight makes it really bad. Fights and disagreements will definitely happen. As an individual you can disagree with your partner over things, and this is very normal and natural. There can't be a real cure for that. What can be done is that the intensity of fights could be kept under control. You have to set some ground rules with your partner, otherwise things can go pretty much out of hand.

4. **The constant fear of infidelity** – The constant fear of infidelity can drive a person mad. Even when your partner stays nearby, you could be a victim of this fear. When he stays miles apart, then it is quite natural for you to be worried. You can have constant thoughts of him being with someone else. Maybe you still don't trust him that much. Or, maybe despite the trust on him, you don't trust the people around him. Though it is natural to have such

thoughts, but you can't let this fear overpower your love for each other. You have to work out a way that keeps you at peace. Imagine if your partner constantly doubts you. It'll make your life hell to a point that you might feel like breaking the relationship. Don't get to that point. Talk about such issues wit your partner. Let him know what you feel, and understand his viewpoints.

5. **Possessiveness** – In any usual relationship, partners do tend to get possessive about each other. In a long distance relationship, the possessiveness is more than usual relationships. When you can't meet your lover regularly, and when you see him spending time with other people, it is natural to get possessive. Though possessiveness is not a negative emotion, but too much of anything is a bad thing. Too much of this emotion can be detrimental for your own good. When you are extremely possessive about your partner, you might get dominating in a wrong way. Nobody likes to get dominated. If your partner does the

same with you, even you wouldn't like it. Ultimately, the relationship will suffer. So, it is advisable to identify this problem in the beginning stages so that the root cause can be eliminated.

6. **Missing each other** – When a vast distance separates you, you can't help but miss each other more often than not. Though technology can help you to stay connected, it can't give you the happiness of physical proximity. Being miles away can make your heart sad. You will miss him in every small and big thing that you do. You will miss him when you see other couples together. Though this is a part and parcel of long distance relationships, you should try to find ways to keep yourself busy. When you miss somebody too much, your emotions get clouded and you are unable to see things with clarity. And, it is imperative for any relationship to have utmost clarity for its own survival.

Chapter 2: Secrets of a Successful Long Distance Relationship

Long distance relationships can be really challenging. A couple has to deal with many more issues than any other normal couple. You might have to deal with your partner's insecurity in addition to yours. There could be spells of doubts and fights. You might get jealous of your lover's friends who get to spend time with him. You may even want to give up because of the unending wait and despair. But, if you love your partner and really want to be with him, then nothing will come in your way. Faith and hope will definitely see you through. All you need is the will to put in your best efforts to make the relationship work. A long distance relationship can definitely work for both of you if you are ready for the upcoming roller coaster ride. Following are few tips and strategies that can help you to understand your lover a little better and to let your relationship grow and prosper in the best way possible:

1. **Establish trust** – Trust has to be the base of any strong relationship. No kind of association can survive unless and until it is built on a firm and solid base of trust. For a relationship like this where distance can bring in differences, there is no way you can survive without trust. You don't want to jeopardize your relationship for your inability to believe in someone. A long distance relationship demands more trust and patience than normal relationships. While in a normal relationship, you have the advantage of seeing each other at will; it does not work this way when the distance is long. You just can't walk into the house of your lover.

   All you can do is believe in him and trust that what he tells you is actually the truth. Give your partner a fair chance. Don't doubt his intentions at every small thing. Don't threaten him that you will break the relationship if he goes for a lunch with someone you don't like. Don't overact or over think on issues. You definitely don't want to break your relationship over a Facebook status that he shared or because you think that the girl in his office flirts with him. Probably it is not what you are thinking. Learn to trust your partner. Establishing and then building trust will go a really long way to bring you guys closer. Though, it takes time to build belief and trust, you have to give yourself and your partner that time. Resolve to see through the wall of doubt and try to go to the root cause of a situation before reacting on anything and everything.

2. **Have patience** – You can't survive a long distance relationship unless you have loads of patience in you. You have to accept the fact that your lover will be spending much of his time with other people. This is but obvious because you are not there with him. You might not

get an immediate reply to your messages or emails because he could be busy somewhere. At such times, it is required of you to display patience and understanding. You can't fight for each message that was delayed. Be more understanding of his situation and also make him realize your situation if need be. If you find your partner being the impatient one, then take it upon yourself to slowly explain to him that patience is the key.

Spending time with each other and getting to know each other is the way to sustain a healthy relationship, but your distance will restrict you from doing so. In such a case you have to have enormous amounts of patience to make do with the phone calls you get to do or the little time you spend with each other. When you feel that you are being ignored and that he has no time for you, stop such negative thoughts from growing. Just divert your mind and get busy with your own life. While the relationship is important, don't make it a reason to cry and brood all the time.

3. **Have a life of your own** – It is very essential that you have a life of your own. Your day should not revolve around your lover. In cases like these, issues get magnified and matters intensify. Have a schedule of your own and also set your priorities right. While it is important that you give your lover enough time, it is unnecessary that you give him all your time. Have your own personal goals in life, be it small or big goals. Have your personal agendas that have nothing to do with your lover.

Also, you should have friends of your own to go out and spend time with. When a person is solely dependent on another person for all his emotional needs, things can get very tricky, especially so when the person is not around. You have to create a little world of your own, where you can sit, relax and introspect on your life. When your partner sees you putting in efforts to achieve your personal goals, he will respect you more as a person. And, it will also secure him that you are not completely dependent on him for you emotional needs.

4. **Encourage open communication** – If there is something that shakes your trust and troubles you, make sure that you discuss it with your partner. While it is important to give the other person some space, sometimes there can be things can trouble you in spite of your efforts. If you ignore all the issues popping in your head, it could be hazardous for the relationship. So, it is better to solve all the real issues by talking them out. Some couples might also consider this step unnecessary because, owing to the long distance, the

couples anyway don't get too much time with each other.

So, they don't want to waste the little time they get brainstorming over problems and issues. But, in the long run, ignoring of issues can be very detrimental for the future of the relationship. Talking about relevant issues and problems is not wasting of time. In fact, it is like an investment that you make for your future. See the larger picture, be reasonable and talk it out. Your partner with also appreciate your transparency, and this will encourage him to be more open with you about other things and issues.

5. **Make an effort to see each other** – Though the distance can restrict you, but you should make sincere efforts to see each other as mush as possible. You can also consider paying your partner a surprise visit. The idea of the trip should be to surprise him and to spend some

quality time with him and not to spy on him. Your partner will definitely appreciate the sincere efforts that you make to see him. Plan your office leaves and family commitments in a way that you get to meet and spend time with your lover more often than not. If the distance is not much, then it will be easier to plan frequent visits, but if the distance is more, then it will be challenging.

See what works out for you. Save some money every month and keep it aside. The amount need not be much. You can spend this money on him when you meet. Pamper him and show him that you really love him. Talk to your partner and let him know that you feel that you guys should see each other as often as possible. If it is really impossible to meet because of work commitments or other issues, then don't spoil your mood and keep the hope alive. Sooner or later, things will work out. Just don't give up, and keep on trying. Your enthusiasm will also motivate your lover to put in his best efforts.

6. **Keep the spark on** – While lovers are really happy and excited in the beginning of their relationship, the spunk seems to die after the initial phase is over. With long distance relationships, it is all the more difficult to keep the fire on. It is important that you make some dedicated efforts from your side to not let this spark die. Always remember at the back of your head the real reason to be together. This reason will motivate you along the way. You need to know in your heart that you guys really love each other. In spite of the distance, what is it that connects the two of you with each other? How much do you love your partner? Why do you want to be with him? The answers to these questions will help you to go through the lonely

times when you miss your partner. Don't let the distance turn you into a boring person.

Do things for him that would be difficult otherwise. You can plan a surprise visit or can also send him surprise gifts. If nothing else you can send him heartfelt emails and letters. These little things will also let your partner know about how much you appreciate him. This will strengthen your bond with your lover, irrespective of the distance that seems to separate you.

7. **Make use of technology** – Life today is much simpler than older times. While, earlier, lovers had to wait for days to receive and send letters, today it is a lot easier to communicate with your loved ones. You should make use of technology as much as possible to stay connected and to be in touch. Work out a time that is suitable for both and talk over the phone about how your day was

and about general things. You can also send frequent emails and e-cards to express your feelings towards your partner. Your partner will definitely appreciate it. You can also download a chat application on your phone to remain in touch constantly.

There are many apps available today that can add a fun element in your chats and emails. Download such apps and make use of them. While most of these apps are free of cost, others are extremely cheap. So, you can actually have lots of fun with minimum amount of money. Browse the internet to know more about the apps that can be useful for the two of you. Learn about the apps, and if they help you to stay connected, then go ahead and download them.

8. **Think and talk about the future** –
   Talking about your future and how you would want it to be will break the monotony of the distance that you guys

experience. Sometimes, you or your lover might find it very difficult to carry on with the relationship. This can make you doubt your own intentions and can discourage you in many ways. At such times, reboot yourself and think about the future that you want. Think about how it would be if you guys can be together in the same place. Think about how it would be if you could see him every day, if you could spend lots of time together.

Imagine yourself with him, having a great time together. Such thoughts will rejuvenate you and remind you of the love that you have in your heart for your lover. Talk about such pleasant thoughts of the future with your partner. Even he would feel happy to know that you think about him in your future plans. It will give him security and happiness. He will appreciate how pleasantly you think about him. This will go a long way in bonding you two together.

9. **Clarity about your end goals** – You should always be clear as to where you see the relationship after a certain point of time. Though, it's difficult to know from the beginning, you'll need some time to figure out where everything is going. But, having a general idea of where and how you want things to be will be helpful. Maybe you want to move to where your partner is after a couple of years. Maybe you want him to shift. Maybe you are or maybe you are not looking at getting married with him.

   Whatever it is, it will be good if you discuss your thoughts and plans with your lover. This will also help your partner and help him to make up his mind on how he wants things to go. This step will help you both in the long run. Just like you can have your insecurities about your long distance relationship, he too can have his insecurities. When you discuss your end goals with him, it will give him a perspective and clarity on the whole thing. No matter where you two end up, it is important to be clear.

10. **Do not go overboard** – Though rules for each relationship would be unique, but it generally is advised to keep things in a limit. Never go overboard. You should do what you feel is right, but never do a thing just to assert a point to the other person. Do not stress yourself too much about the long distance. When you stress yourself, you'll automatically do everything you can to show your partner that the distance does not matter and that you love him. While expressing love and putting in efforts for each other is important and is recommended, but you might spoil things if you overdo things.

So, while calling him twice or thrice a day might be a good idea to keep the communication on, calling ten times in a day might make it weird and difficult for you in the long run. Doing the wrong things can show how insecure and messed up you are, and this can irritate the other person. You definitely don't want to do this. So, remember to put in the right amount of efforts to keep things happy, but stop yourself from going overboard.

11. **Be yourself** – Generally, when couples who live away from each other get to spend a weekend or a few days together, the entire time goes away in being your best self. When you don't get to see your partner for days, then you definitely don't want to lose the little time that you might get together. This is quite a natural thing, but on the other hand, a relationship is more about being able to be together through the regular, mundane stuff of everyday. So, you should try and be yourself. Make it a

point to spend some regular time with your lover, where you two do nothing fancy but something simple, such as cooking a meal together and going for a walk.

Keep special and fancy stuff for sometimes, but concentrate more on the mundane stuff because that is your real test. If you can survive a boring day with your partner, without really getting bored, then this relationship is for you. Simple and regular things like these will help you to get a better understanding of your partner, which will definitely be extremely helpful in for the future of your relationship. And, this realization that your partner and you are great together will motivate you through the days when you guys are apart. It will keep you and your partner going.

Chapter 3: Tips to Cope with Loneliness

A long distance relationship can make you miss your partner more often than not. Your friends might be busy with their partners leaving you with no option but to miss your partner more. Even if your friends are there for you, they can't take the place of your partner. You would find yourself missing him in all the small and big things. This can make you really lonely. While you miss him and wish to meet him, there is something that you can constructively do with your loneliness. Though missing each other is fine, but too much loneliness can lead to a dangerous idleness, where you sit and over think about issues. This is not a great thing to do. If you are idle, you might sit and cook up stories in your head. These stories could be extremely dangerous for your relationship. So, it is better to fight the loneliness off. The following strategies can help you do so:

1. **Catching up with old friends** – There might be many of your friends that you haven't met in a long time because of different schedules and other commitments. Now could be a good time to catch up with old friends. Try calling them up and meeting them. Make plans with them and know more about what is happening in their lives. This time when you are without your lover can be a good time to rekindle some old and lost friendships. Even if your friends are busy with their own relationships and other personal stuff, they'll appreciate that you made a real effort to catch up with them. If you don't have many such friends in your town, then call up your old friends and have a nice chat with them. Reconnecting with old buddies is always a heartwarming thing to do.

2. **Spending time with the family** – In the absence of your lover, you can

consider spending more time with your family. Make plans to visit your family more often than before, and if they are nearby then it'll be easier to do so. While your family will appreciate it, you will not feel lonely and would get to enjoy the love of your family. If your lover's family is in town and if he is okay with it, then you can consider spending time with them also. They might also miss him a lot, and you could share their pain. This will bring you closer to them, which in turn is good for your relationship with your partner. And, even he would be relieved that his family is being taken care of.

3. **Watching sitcoms and movies** - Catch up on your favorite sitcoms or movies. This alone time of yours can actually turn into a boon for you because you can catch up on all the things you had earlier lost out on. This can be a really fun thing to do over the weekends

and holidays. There might be many movies you wanted to watch but could not watch because of various reasons. Make use of the time when you are away from your lover and watch those movies. You could have many favorite sitcoms and movies that you can consider re-watching. Take a big bucket of popcorn and binge watch all that you love.

4. **Getting busy in work** – Immerse yourself in your work. Make a daily schedule of what you want to achieve in a day and get at it. You could be doing any kind of work, just focus more than ever. Make this time an opportunity to excel in your professional life. Personal life is also important, but right now you can concentrate more on your profession. Spend more number of hours working, if you can do that. Even if you don't spend extra hours on your work, make sure that your determination, will and focus is much

more than otherwise. This will help you accomplish more in less amount of time. Help others at work. Do things that are out of your comfort zone.

5. **Finding support in your best buddies** - Call your best buddies and cook a nice meal for them. Plan movie nights or throw a party for them. This will surprise them and bring them closer to you. Having happy relationships in your life will keep your spirit high and uplifted. You should talk about how you feel about being all alone and about what you think of your partner. Talk about things that disturb you and about your insecurities. Your best buddies will understand you and will show you the right way. They want your happiness and peace of mind to remain intact, so they will be more than happy to help.

6. **Joining a gym or health club** - You can consider joining a health club or yoga class. This will keep you occupied

and healthy also. While a gym will help you sweat it out, a health club will offer you many more facilities. Make a list of all the available gyms and health clubs around your place and their price range. Now, see what suits you and your budget. Take a membership as soon as possible and make it a point to go there every alternate day, if not every day. If you want to save your money, you can also look at going for daily walks at a neighborhood park. This could be a really cost free way to stay healthy and happy. Think of what suits you the best and just get at it.

7. **Starting a hobby** - Re-starting old hobbies can be a good option to beat loneliness. You should think about going back to a hobby that you might have had in your teens or maybe a few years ago. If it is feasible to work on it again, then you should definitely go ahead. You can also look for new options. Make a list of

new things that you can learn. Try a few of them and see what works for you. Even if you devote a few hours every week for your hobby, it is more than enough. As long as you have something good and constructive that keeps your mind and body occupied, it is great.

8. **Indulging the senses in a creative way** – Creative channels and various art forms are great ways to keep the mind occupied and soul happy. You should definitely consider expressing yourself through various creative ways. You can write a journal or write poetry if that interests you. Join a writing club in your vicinity to meet other budding writers. You can also join a painting or drawing club. Painting is also a great way to express your inner self. It is a beautiful art form and you should give it a try.

9. **Joining a social club** – You can also consider on joining a social club. You will get to meet many new people at

such places. Meeting new people and getting to know them can be a great way of warding off your loneliness. You can join various food groups if you enjoy going out and eating. These clubs organize get-togethers every now and then to explore a new eating place. This can be a great way of utilizing your time.Clubs that indulge in social causes can be a great option. You can work for a cause with these clubs and give your time for the betterment of others. Look for your options. You should do anything that makes you feel good and content.

10. **Scheduling your time** – If you schedule your day well, you would have little time to get bored, which in turn will help you not to miss your partner too much. Sit for a few minutes every day and think about the agenda for the day. Make a schedule for the day, and make necessary changes as and when

the need arises. Make tentative schedules for the week ahead. This will help you to get an idea what lies ahead of you. Make it a point to schedule your time well to include time for both work and personal refreshment.

11. **Pampering your self** – Leave no opportunity to pamper yourself. Each one's idea of pampering oneself can be different. Figure out what you enjoy the most and go and do it. Maybe you want to go for a spa or a nice and trendy hair cut. If you enjoy swimming, you can go for swimming every weekend or on alternate days. The idea is to show yourself some love and care. If you don't want to go for an expensive spa, go for a cheaper one. But, do take out some time and money for yourself. Even if you pamper yourself once in a few months, it would be great. You need your love and attention more than anyone else does.

Conclusion

Thank you again for purchasing this book!

I hope this book was able to help you in dealing with the various problems and issues that arise while being in a long distance relationship. A long distance relationship is difficult than a usual relationship because every small issue gets magnified. Due to the lack of communication and insecurity, the lovers start doubting each other. Because you can't see your lover as often as you would like to, you might easily get frustrated and irritated. Such behavioral changes can affect the relationship in a negative way. You can put your lover off, and due to the distance it is all the more difficult to solve issues.

This book can be your guide to foresee the issues that generally affect a long distance relationship. The secrets of a successful long distance relationship can help you to give in your best efforts for the relationship.

Finally, if you found this book useful, please take the time to share your thoughts and post a review on Amazon. It'd be greatly appreciated!

Thank you and good luck!

Made in the USA
Monee, IL
06 November 2020